What You See!

Diana Bentley

Contents

Fish 2
Frog 3
Butterfly 4
Spider 5
Snake 6
Owl 7

OXFORD

UNIVERSITY PRESS

Can you see the fish?

Can you see the frog?

Can you see the butterfly?

Can you see the spider?

Can you see the snake?

Can you see the owl?

What can you see?